Library of Congress Cataloging-in-Publication Data
Thrive! : devotions for students.
    p. cm.
  ISBN 978-0-7586-1507-7
  1. Christian teenagers--Religious life. I. Concordia Publishing
House.
  BV4531.3.T47 2008
  242'.63--dc22
                              2008028890

1   2   3   4   5   6   7   8   9   10   17   16   15   14   13   12   11   10   09   08

THRIVE!

Devotions for Students

CONCORDIA PUBLISHING HOUSE • SAINT LOUIS

Dedicated to **teens** around the **world** living for **Christ** and learning daily how to thrive.

Special thanks to all those who helped to make this vision a reality. First and foremost, thanks and praise be to God our Father and the Lord Jesus Christ for taking this project farther than anyone could have imagined.

Next, thanks to Doug Doellinger, Gary Doede, Irene Giguere, and Melissa Weldon, advisers for the Christus Honors program at Baltimore Lutheran School, Baltimore, Maryland, for the opportunity to make this devotional book happen.

Thanks also to Samira Laniyan and Jessica Cundiff for their help in publicizing this project. Thanks to Jane Austin, Rebecca Bartlet, Russell Davies, Gary Fritz, Todd Nitz, Sarah Poertner, and Jennifer Roettjer for helping to compile the devotions, and thanks also to their students, without whom this book never would have been possible. In addition, thanks to Rev. James Sharp and Rev. Jason Wolter for editing these devotions for theological accuracy and soundness.

Thanks to Pamela Post for her belief and support in this project from day one and for her editing help. Thanks to Dave Post and Baltimore Lutheran School for supporting this project both in prayer and financially. Thanks to my brother, David Post, for the use of the computer.

Finally, thanks to family, friends, and fellow brothers and sisters in Christ who prayed for and supported this project the whole way through—this is for you!

Jocelyn

Special Thanks to Our Teen Authors

Dottie Avery

Kurt McKenna

Branden Barrera

Hannah Muther

Mikaela Barz

Heather Nagel

Adam Behmlander

Andrea Newkirk

Christa Bemis

Abby Newman

Paul Canales

Candice Noelker

Anna Cloeter

Kelly Osborn

Shalimar Davis

Micah Owens

Cody Deaton

Ryan Permison

Kevin Dempsey

Liz Peterson

Amy Dowdle

Leah Rayner

Audrey Fikes

Ian Reynolds

Samantha Flores

Katie Rieckers

Mary Garant

Stephanie Roach

H. T. Girmay

Emilie Rupp

Eric Gramenz

Kristina Russie

Michael Healy

Eric Schepman

Jacob Hercamp

Layna Schneider

Karina Heredia

Tom Schroer

Jon Hernandez

Elisabeth Shearier

Melanie Jackson

Ryan Stein

Miranda Jackson

Christina Velasquez

Kailyn Liefer

Krista Wegener

Jacob Mayer

JD Zischke

Let grain abound throughout the land; on the tops of the hills may it sway. Let its fruit flourish like Lebanon; let it thrive like the grass of the field.

Psalm 72:16 (NIV)

Anonymous

Sola Gratia

Read: Ephesians 2:49

Imagine that your teacher's son is in all of your classes, and he never gets anything wrong on any homework, tests, or anything! Now imagine that you always get a zero on all of your homework. Naturally, you might start to hate that "perfect" kid.

After the last test before the final, your English teacher announces everyone's grades to the class. He says that his son scored a zero on the test. In fact, he was the only one in the class who had less than 100 percent on the test. As you look at him and sneer, you see that he is smiling. Then, you look at your test and realize that it is not written in your handwriting, but in his. After the semester final, you see your grades and notice that all of your zeros have been replaced with a perfect score of 100 percent. The teacher's son called you and told you that at his father's urging, he rewrote all of his classmates' homework so that it was perfect,

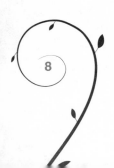

even though they had all failed. He did this gladly, even though his classmates had picked on him.

God works the same way. Just substitute "teacher" with God, "son" with Jesus, and the failing grades with sin. Because of our sinful nature, we despised God. But even while we hated Him, He loved us and forgave us. We are saved entirely by His grace. This was His will: to love and save us, even though we did nothing to deserve it.

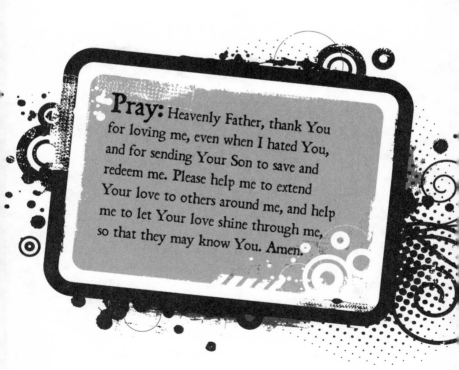

Pray: Heavenly Father, thank You for loving me, even when I hated You, and for sending Your Son to save and redeem me. Please help me to extend Your love to others around me, and help me to let Your love shine through me, so that they may know You. Amen.

Hannah Muther

Running the Race

Read: Hebrews 12:1–2

It is the day of gym class everyone dreads: *running the mile*. You probably know the feeling—the day is coming, and every day you hope it is not today. Inevitably, the day arrives.

What's the big deal about running the mile? The track seems to just keep going and going, with no end in sight, but you know you cannot quit. You have to keep going until you have finished the race and met your goal. It takes endurance, perseverance, and hard work.

The Bible often compares our lives to running a race. Hebrews 12:1 says, "Therefore, since we are surrounded by so great a cloud of witnesses, let us also lay aside every weight, and sin which clings so closely, and let us run with endurance the

race that is set before us." In our lives, it's easy to pretend that all we have to do is the fifty-yard dash. We tell ourselves that high school is all about having fun and enjoying the best years of our life. But in actuality, this is only a small part of a long race, with a finish line that lies beyond our earthly lives. This race takes perseverance and endurance. It is so easy to want to give up or to be distracted and lose our focus. In gym class, there is usually a friend cheering you on as you run. The same is true in life. We have a Friend who has already run the race in record time, and He loves you even when you stumble.

The best part about this race, unlike gym class, is the prize. Timothy says, "I have fought the good fight, I have finished the race, I have kept the faith. Henceforth there is laid up for me the crown of righteousness, which the Lord, the righteous judge, will award me on that Day" (2 Timothy 4:7–8). We have the ultimate reward for finishing the race faithfully: heaven. The next time you feel like quitting, remember that there is One who runs with us and for us. He has provided a reward that we receive at the end of our earthly race. Let that joyful hope give you the strength to keep running.

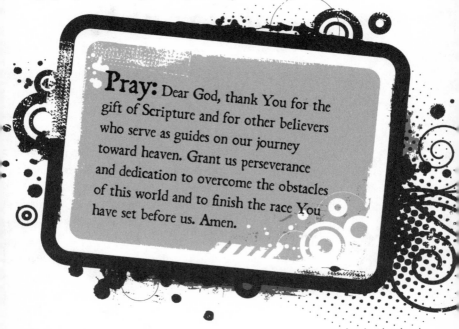

Pray: Dear God, thank You for the gift of Scripture and for other believers who serve as guides on our journey toward heaven. Grant us perseverance and dedication to overcome the obstacles of this world and to finish the race You have set before us. Amen.

Christina
Velasquez

Times
of Trouble

Read: Psalm 46:1

Trouble, hardships, hurt, and pain: these things daily plague our lives because of sin. We often find ourselves in tough situations, searching for a solution that, by ourselves, we cannot find. So many times we are totally caught up in the heat of the moment, trying to figure out what is wrong and how to solve the problem, that we completely forget that there is always someone there to help us.

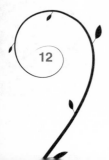

During eighth grade, I went through something that changed my life forever. Like every other normal day, my mom had dropped me off at school. But this wasn't going to be a normal day. At lunch, I was called to the office and told that I was to leave early. A family friend picked me up and took me home. When I got there, my dad told me the devastating news: my mom had suddenly passed away. I cried for hours and hours until I could cry no more. How? Why? I had seen her less than five hours earlier. I couldn't believe she was gone.

That was two-and-a-half years ago. There is no way that I could ever have gotten through that time in my life without the help of God. I was surrounded and encouraged by so many Christians. I was blessed by all the people God had put into my life. In that time of trouble when I needed a place to take refuge, God was there, guiding and protecting me every step of the way. I understood that although it is not what I wanted to happen, God was still a good God, and He knew how to take care of me.

So many times in our lives when we are going through something difficult, we try to fix it on our own. We think that we can work it all out and everything will be okay. When it doesn't work out that way, some people even turn away from God in their anger. This is not how it should be. We need to remember that God is on our side. He wants what is best for us, and He will take care of us. In every situation, He is our "refuge and strength, a very present help in trouble" (Psalm 46:1).

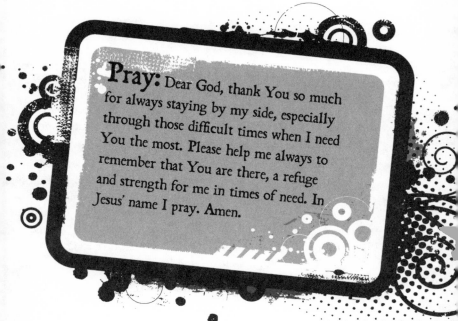

Pray: Dear God, thank You so much for always staying by my side, especially through those difficult times when I need You the most. Please help me always to remember that You are there, a refuge and strength for me in times of need. In Jesus' name I pray. Amen.

Mary Garant

Stress

Read: 2 Corinthians 4:16

Today's world is very stressful. Teenagers seem to have way too much on their plates. We have school, sports, after-school activities, homework, and we still have to find time to have a social life. Personally, I know sometimes it feels like the world just will not give me a break.

Paul writes in 2 Corinthians 4:16, "So we do not lose heart. Though our outer self is wasting away, our inner self is being renewed day by day." I like to read this verse when I am stressed out. When I feel like life will not cut me a break, I can just stop and read this verse. It comforts me to know that God is with me and renewing me every day. Even when I feel tired and stressed out, I know God is with me, and He will help me through my difficult days.

So if you are ever stressed out with school, sports, or any of the million other things life seems to throw your way, just stop, take a deep breath, and read this short verse. It is amazing how simply reading a short verse can help you through the rest of your difficult day.

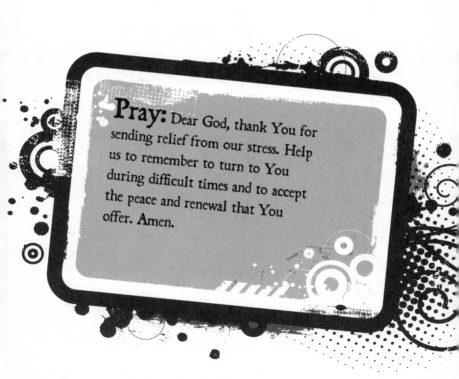

Pray: Dear God, thank You for sending relief from our stress. Help us to remember to turn to You during difficult times and to accept the peace and renewal that You offer. Amen.

Dottie Avery

Fending off the Lion

Read: 1 Peter 5:8–9

Ever feel like that homework is too much to bear, or that project is never going to get done? What about something a little more serious? Have you ever felt like you will never be able to live without that boy or girl you like, or you will never live if your parents go through with that divorce they have been talking about? How can you get through the rest of your life without your grandparent who passed away?

The truth is that trials and difficult situations will continue to come up throughout the rest of our lives. We have two choices as to how to deal with these hard times: we can give in to sin and wallow in sadness, blocking out all the good that is in our lives; or with God's help we can resist Satan and keep putting our faith

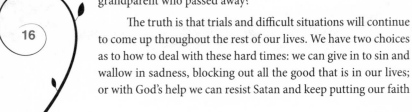

in Christ's promises. Satan is constantly lurking around like a lion, trying to find a weak spot in our lives that he can take advantage of and make us question our faith and question God.

We do not need to be discouraged by things that do not go the way we would like. By faith, we know that Jesus went through the same kinds of suffering when He was on earth, and He understands how we feel. He knows how hard it is for us to go through the temptations and sins we experience every day. We can also be encouraged to know that there are other people in the world who know what we are going through, whom God sends to help us when our load becomes unbearable.

Next time you feel like you are at the end of your rope, have faith in Jesus, knowing He is right there with you, helping you in everything you experience and comforting you with His love.

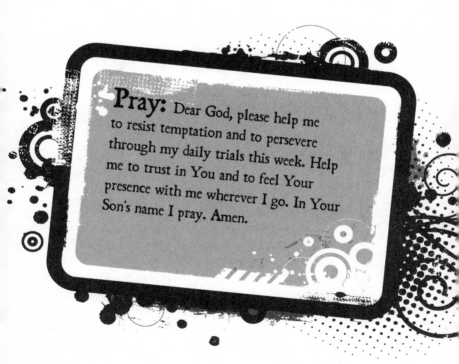

Pray: Dear God, please help me to resist temptation and to persevere through my daily trials this week. Help me to trust in You and to feel Your presence with me wherever I go. In Your Son's name I pray. Amen.

Kelly Osborn

For Love or Money?

Read: Matthew 6:24

How many times a day do we say that we need something? We need more money. We need more stuff. We need more friends, time, and so forth. But what do we really need?

Too many times we try to use God for our earthly benefit. Then, when we get what we want, we turn our backs on Him and devote our lives to the things of this world that He has given us rather than to God Himself. We may not even notice it, but generally we center our lives on material things. Really, the best things in life, such as love, friendship, and especially God's love for us, cannot be bought with money. When Jesus was confronted by some townspeople about whether or not they should pay taxes, Jesus told them, "Render to Caesar the things

that are Caesar's" (Matthew 22:21). Because Caesar's face was on the coin, it belonged to him; it was of the world. So we are to give to the world what belongs to the world and give to God what belongs to God.

Matthew 6:24 explains that what it comes down to is whether you trust God with everything in your life or if you trust yourself and the world. Will you invest yourself in the eternal God or in the temporary things of this finite world? "But as for me and my house, we will serve the LORD" (Joshua 24:15).

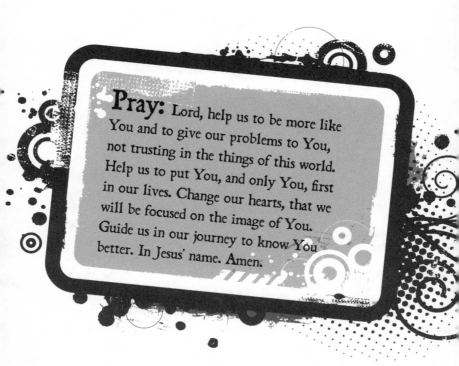

Pray: Lord, help us to be more like You and to give our problems to You, not trusting in the things of this world. Help us to put You, and only You, first in our lives. Change our hearts, that we will be focused on the image of You. Guide us in our journey to know You better. In Jesus' name. Amen.

Kailyn Liefer

My Best Friend

Read: Romans 6:8

When I was ten years old, my mother was diagnosed with cancer. Divorced with three children, she had no emotional or physical support. While she was being treated, she also had no faith in the Lord. Three days before my twelfth birthday, she went into remission. After that, she started taking my oldest brother and me to church, and she confessed her faith in Christ as her Savior. One year later, we moved to Colorado. My mom got married and was finally happy.

Only two months after getting married, Mom had a checkup and was diagnosed with cancer once again. This time, it was a very rare form of cancer for someone her age. She went through chemotherapy and radiation again, but it only made

things worse. When she accepted the fact that she was not going to go into remission, she went to a well-known hospice center in Boca Raton, Florida, where she passed away on February 14, 2004. The last memory I have of my mother being happy is when she said to me that knowing Christ was the best thing in her life, and that Christ would be with her forever. My mother knew and rejoiced that she would be with her Lord for eternity as He promised in Romans 6:8.

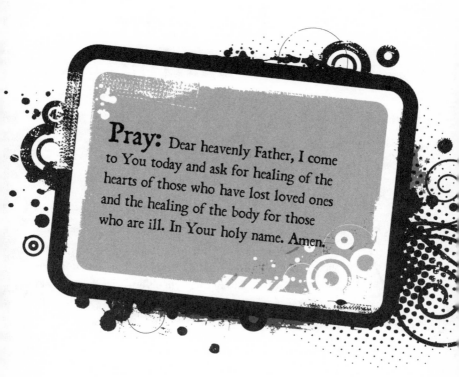

Pray: Dear heavenly Father, I come to You today and ask for healing of the hearts of those who have lost loved ones and the healing of the body for those who are ill. In Your holy name. Amen.

Micah Owens

No More Boasting

Read: Genesis 37:7

Nathan was an all-star athlete. He was the captain and MVP of the basketball team, as well as the leading scorer. His team went all the way to the semifinals of the state tourney. The baseball coach also named him the captain of the baseball team.

One day at practice, Nathan started bragging about all the college scouts who were coming to watch him play in the big game on Saturday. "Two Big Ten schools are driving all this way to watch me play," he warned, "so you better not mess it up." The other boys on the team were tired of hearing it. Ever since they had been freshmen, all they heard was how great Nathan was, even from the coach.

Jeremy, another boy on the team, spoke up, "I would

laugh if he couldn't play on Saturday. Then what would all those scouts think?" The other boys agreed. "Maybe we could put Mrs. Taylor's answer book in his locker," Jeremy suggested. The boys all seemed to think it was a good idea. "If all the teachers think he cheated on his pre-calc test, then Nathan wouldn't be eligible to play in the game Saturday."

Finally, Andrew, the first baseman, spoke up, "Guys, just let it go. I want to win Saturday." After thinking it over, they all agreed with Andy. They shrugged it off and started their warm-up.

Sometimes we are like Nathan, and sometimes we are like Jeremy. God has blessed all of us with many gifts, but sometimes we boast about them. Other times we get jealous or angry with others, just as Joseph's brothers were with him. Thankfully, God forgives us all our sins, through the death and resurrection of His Son, Jesus. Now we know that when our earthly life comes to an end, our eternal heavenly life will begin.

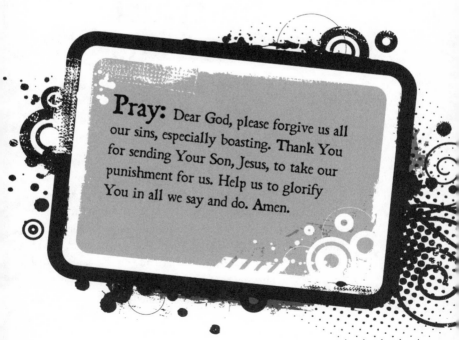

Pray: Dear God, please forgive us all our sins, especially boasting. Thank You for sending Your Son, Jesus, to take our punishment for us. Help us to glorify You in all we say and do. Amen.

Kevin Dempsey

Spiritual Character

Read: Exodus 32

Webster's dictionary defines the word *character* as "the combination of qualities or features that distinguishes one person, group, or thing from another." In other words, your character is what makes you different from everyone else. A popular layman defines character as "who you are when no one is looking." This means that you act the way in private as you do in public. When Christ is in your heart, you also adopt a special "spiritual character," or how you act within your relationship with God.

The Israelites didn't demonstrate very good spiritual character. After they had been miraculously delivered from slavery by God's own hand, they decided to rebuke Moses because he had been up on the mountain talking to God for a while. Theirs was a superficial faith. They confessed that God could do anything after witnessing the many miracles He performed on their behalf, but then they turned from God to their own golden idols. To make matters worse, they gave the credit for their freedom to the golden calf, saying, "These are your gods, O Israel, who brought you up out of the land of Egypt!" (Exodus 32:4).

God was furious at this display of blasphemy. He was so mad at the Israelites that He was on the verge of killing them on the spot. Moses stepped in, however, and talked God into showing them mercy. Because of their horrible spiritual character, "the Lord sent a plague on the people, because they made the calf, the one that Aaron made" (Exodus 32:35).

As sinners, we do not always have strong spiritual character. Often, when we wander away from God by neglecting prayer and His Word, we tend to take a step back in our spiritual walk with God. Too often, we make our own "golden calves" and put them before God.

Thankfully, we have our own "Moses" to intercede for us when we screw up in the eyes of God. This is His Son, Jesus, who pleads for us with His own blood. He willingly subjected Himself to unbearable torture and execution to pay for our sin. For His sake, God has delivered us to an eternal promised land—heaven. As we receive this gift in faith, God strengthens our spiritual character so that we might walk closer with Him in this world.

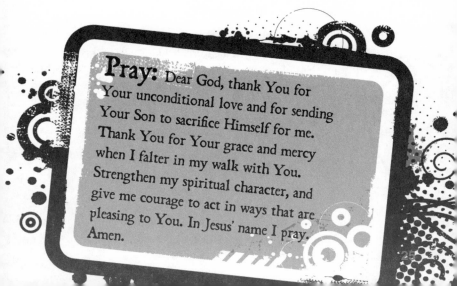

Pray: Dear God, thank You for Your unconditional love and for sending Your Son to sacrifice Himself for me. Thank You for Your grace and mercy when I falter in my walk with You. Strengthen my spiritual character, and give me courage to act in ways that are pleasing to You. In Jesus' name I pray. Amen.

Christa Bemis

Living Out the Law

Read: Romans 13:1–2

26

Teens all around the world tend to enjoy testing the limits and rules of society and their parents. The reasons range from our need for attention to the need to be a part of the "cool" crowd to just our sinful desire to break the rules. But God has put these laws into place for a reason, and breaking the laws of a parent or anyone else is also breaking the Law of God.

Not long ago, my sister, Lexus, started developing bad habits and hanging out with the wrong crowd. She lived with my dad and me, and she always tried to push the boundaries he had established. Lexus became what is often called the "wild child" of the family. She was thirteen years old, but she hung out with my high school friends. This is how I came to learn of my sister's drug abuse. Lexus was smoking almost every Friday night with her friends. Although her drug abuse had not yet become habitual, I was still upset. She knew how touchy the subject of drugs was for my dad and me, and still she smoked behind our backs. Due to a family history of drug, alcohol, and rebellion-type issues, this scared me. Yet, my dad didn't seem to notice. Despite my constant badgering about her friends, where she was going, what she was doing, my dad seemed completely oblivious.

When I confronted Lexus, she blatantly lied about the situation. But after realizing she could not get out of the situation, she confessed. I screamed and yelled, and she cried, begging me not to tell Dad. I did not say anything to him then, but later when I found out she had started again, I hinted to my dad that his daughter may be spinning out of control, especially at her young age. After she failed a drug test, she swore never to do it again. When we sat Lexus down to tell her why drugs were such a big deal, especially in our family, she realized what our family had been through. She asked for and received our forgiveness. While the Bible may not say, "Do not do drugs," God gives parents and government officials the authority to say this. Breaking their rules is the same as breaking the rules of God, and that lesson is something my sister learned the hard way.

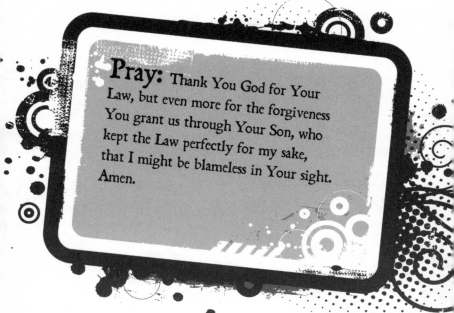

Pray: Thank You God for Your Law, but even more for the forgiveness You grant us through Your Son, who kept the Law perfectly for my sake, that I might be blameless in Your sight. Amen.

JD Zischke

Love

Read: Ephesians 5:1–2

People often copy their parents. They look like their mom or walk like their dad. People say, "You are just like your mother," or "You remind me of your dad."

The Bible says you should be like God. You are God's child; act like your Father. Of course, you cannot do all things just like God, but one thing you can do like Him is show love. He lives love. He forgives freely. He asks you to do the same. Forgive freely. Act in kindness. Show tenderness and live in love.

Ephesians 5:1–2 encourages us to imitate, or copy, God. Through such imitation, people will be reminded of your heavenly Father through you.

Pray: Dear God, thank You for being our Father. Help us to love others as You love them, in everything we do, so that people will see You through us. Amen.

Ian Reynolds

Biblical Self-Esteem

Read: Colossians 2:6–7

Everyone has self-esteem. Sometimes it is low and sometimes it is high.

As stated in Webster's dictionary, self-esteem is "belief in one's self or self-respect." Based on God's view of us, we should have high self-esteem. We, as Christians, also can help raise other people's self-esteem as we treat them as the precious, wonderful people God created them to be.

Low self-esteem is caused by a bad self-image, which is often inflicted by those people around someone. For example, when a person is made fun of at a young age, he may feel worse about himself. On the other hand, with good friends, your self-esteem can become higher as they surround you with their love and support. We need to remember that God has created each of us. As we see ourselves and others through our Savior's eyes, we will think the best about one another and ourselves.

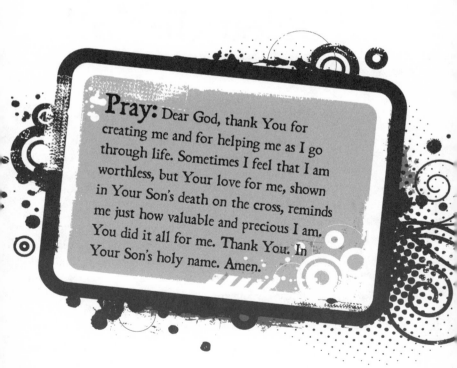

Pray: Dear God, thank You for creating me and for helping me as I go through life. Sometimes I feel that I am worthless, but Your love for me, shown in Your Son's death on the cross, reminds me just how valuable and precious I am. You did it all for me. Thank You. In Your Son's holy name. Amen.

Jacob Hercamp

Hear the Call

Read: 2 Timothy 4:2

The world we live in today is one that does not listen to its Creator. It has been that way since man's fall into sin. It began in the Garden of Eden with Adam and Eve. God told them not to eat of the tree of the knowledge of good and evil. But instead of listening to Him, they chose to listen to the serpent.

Things haven't changed. Many people say there is no God, or they act as though they are gods themselves. These false ideas have spread far and wide. Paul wrote this passage to Timothy to warn him about these false teachings and to encourage him to make sure everything he taught and preached agreed with what the Bible said. We, too, must beware of these false teachings, just as Timothy was, and be prepared to give proper responses.

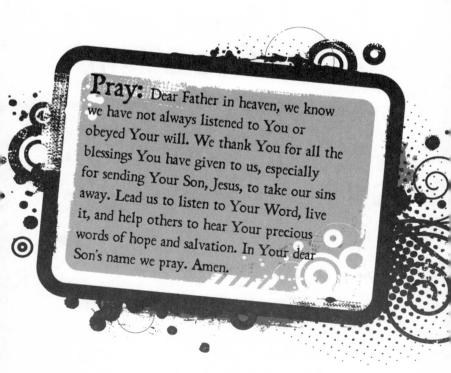

Pray: Dear Father in heaven, we know we have not always listened to You or obeyed Your will. We thank You for all the blessings You have given to us, especially for sending Your Son, Jesus, to take our sins away. Lead us to listen to Your Word, live it, and help others to hear Your precious words of hope and salvation. In Your dear Son's name we pray. Amen.

Stephanie Roach

The Game of Christianity

Read: Philippians 3:12–14

Is there a connection between Christ and sports? Does playing for your high school basketball team have anything to do with growing closer to God? It may not seem like it, but one could actually feed into the other.

What is the point of a basketball game if not to win the game? To win the game, you have to train, have a goal in mind, and strive to accomplish that goal. Can you see a similarity now? In many ways, Christianity is just one basketball game after another.

Let's look at this analogy more closely. First, there is the training. Before you can actually play a game of basketball, you want to know what you are doing and that you are getting better.

Being a Christian involves training. To train as a Christian, you need to read and study God's Word to be a good representative of the faith. Then you have your teammates, people who work together to try to score baskets, make plays, and reach the goal. As Christians, our faith community is our team. We are, together, the Body of Christ. We help each other in good times and in bad times. We are always pushing and encouraging one another.

The most important part of basketball, though, is the game itself. Those fast thirty-two minutes of play are what the training is for. What the team does with those minutes determines the outcome. We, as Christians, are here for a brief time. In that time, we make bad choices (fouls), and we make good choices (3-pointers). No matter how well or badly we play, we always remember that our time is short, and we must work as hard as we can that we may, when the buzzer sounds, have lived lives worthy of the name of Christ. Best of all, and unlike basketball, we know how this game ends. Jesus has already won the victory for us, and through His merits we receive the prize—eternal life with our God.

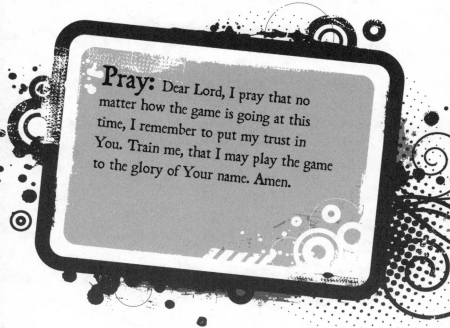

Pray: Dear Lord, I pray that no matter how the game is going at this time, I remember to put my trust in You. Train me, that I may play the game to the glory of Your name. Amen.

Whoever trusts in his riches will fall, but the righteous will thrive like a green leaf.

Proverbs 11:28 (NIV)

Ryan Stein

Riding the Bull

Read: Romans 16:17

In this verse, God tells us that in our everyday lives we have things or people that are obstacles in our paths of righteousness. My grandpa once told me that life was like riding a bull. There will be times when it will kick you off and make you bite the dust. But through Jesus Christ, we can get through our troubles and get right back on the bull for another ride.

God tells us to watch out for those evildoers who try to harm us. We are sinful and constantly fall short of the glory of God. The Gospel is the Good News that we are forgiven and restored through Jesus Christ. This verse tells us that there will be people and things in our way that will try to lead us astray from God and His love, yet we know that God will guide us and lead us safely home.

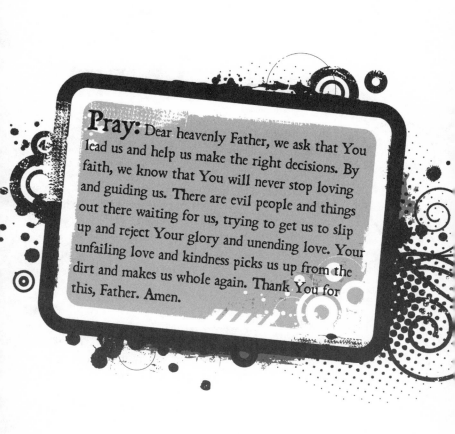

Pray: Dear heavenly Father, we ask that You lead us and help us make the right decisions. By faith, we know that You will never stop loving and guiding us. There are evil people and things out there waiting for us, trying to get us to slip up and reject Your glory and unending love. Your unfailing love and kindness picks us up from the dirt and makes us whole again. Thank You for this, Father. Amen.

H. T. Girmay

Give Thanks

Read: Ephesians 5:20

Have you ever gotten something good without knowing you were getting it? Have you ever met a stranger who helps you a lot? Have you prayed to God and gotten the answer you were looking for? I have gotten all this with my helper, Jesus Christ, who always wants what is best for me and for me to be His follower. I give thanks to God for all He gives me and for helping me to live.

I grew up in Ethiopia, which is one of the scariest countries to live in these days. I came to the U.S. about three years ago because of educational opportunities and better living conditions. I had been praying for these things for years, so I give thanks to God for answering my prayers and leading me to achieve my goal.

Everything we see in the world, and even everything we cannot see, was created by God. Our family and friends are given to us by God, so let us give thanks to God the Father for giving us everything we need. God gave His Son to save us from evil, so let's give thanks and pray to God. Whenever you get something such as a radio, television, CD player, or computer, these are extra things given to you by God. Also, your abilities in athletics, art, teaching, learning, and anything else you can think of are given to you by God. Let us give God thanks for all He has done!

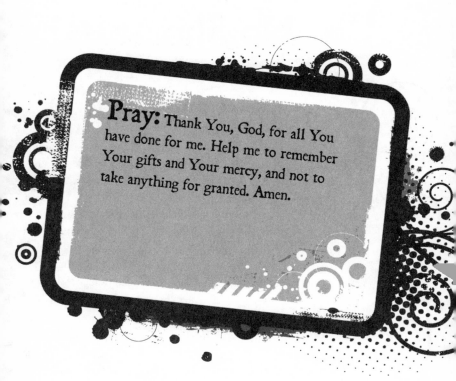

Pray: Thank You, God, for all You have done for me. Help me to remember Your gifts and Your mercy, and not to take anything for granted. Amen.

Layna Schneider

No Shortcuts

Read: Matthew 7:13–14

The Pilgrim's Progress, written by the Christian author John Bunyan, is a book that depicts the struggles and blessings that Christians encounter in their walk of life. The main character, Christian, is determined to make it to the Celestial City. Christian knows that the only way to the Celestial City is through the narrow gate. After Christian passes through the gate, he encounters two men named Formalist and Hypocrisy. Christian asks the men why they did not come through the gate. They replied that it was too far out of the way, and that they decided to take a shortcut by climbing over the wall. Later the two men take the roads of Danger and Destruction and are lost forever.

Many times in our lives, we find ourselves behaving like Formalist and Hypocrisy. We want to take the easy way, even if it is not the right way. Sometimes we take shortcuts by cheating on a test or lying to get out of situations. In the end, our actions betray us. Even if we are not caught for cheating this time, we will still fail the final exam. When we lie, we have to lie even more to keep the first lie going, and soon we are found out. We learn the hard way that the right path is always the best, even if it is not the easiest.

The same holds true for the path to heaven. Many people think that there are multiple ways to get there. Some people become conceited and question being a Christian when times get rough. They want to find an easier way to live and be happy. God tells us that the only way to heaven is through Jesus Christ. Jesus is our gate to salvation, because without Him there is no way to enter heaven. Thankfully, Jesus has experienced all the trials of life and knows what we are going through. God warns us that there will be troubles in this life for us too, but Jesus is always with us. Our reward in heaven outweighs the troubles of this earthly life. Jesus did the impossible for us and made possible the gift of eternal life. There is no need for dangerous or easy shortcuts. Jesus has already paved the way to heaven for us.

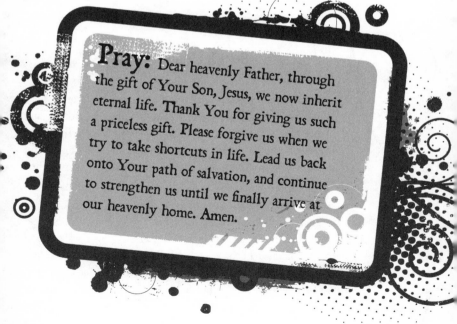

Pray: Dear heavenly Father, through the gift of Your Son, Jesus, we now inherit eternal life. Thank You for giving us such a priceless gift. Please forgive us when we try to take shortcuts in life. Lead us back onto Your path of salvation, and continue to strengthen us until we finally arrive at our heavenly home. Amen.

Jon Hernandez

Mercy

Read: Habakkuk 3:2

"In wrath remember mercy" is a good quote to have hanging on your fridge or pinned to your bulletin board. Because of original sin, there is a lot of anger in people's hearts. Therefore, we need to be reminded constantly of our need to be merciful towards others rather than holding on to our anger against them.

The definition of mercy is "a disposition to be kind and forgiving." If only everyone had a heart full of mercy, the world would be a better place. Maybe we would not have war; maybe there would be no murder or violence. But the world is not like that. Because of man's fall into sin, our world is one full of violence, hate, and war. But believe it or not, you can make a difference.

When you are merciful to others, you spread God's love and compassion to them. You are showing others that you care and want to help them. You are making things better through your merciful actions. Most important, our world is changed as God's love is shown through us to others. That's the power of His love.

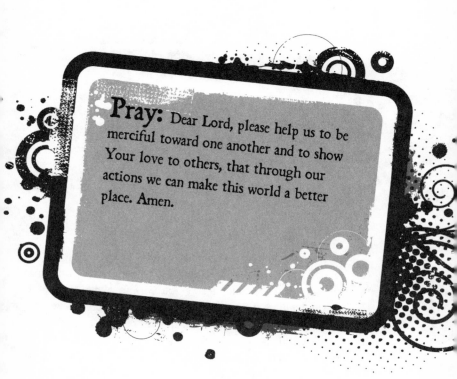

Pray: Dear Lord, please help us to be merciful toward one another and to show Your love to others, that through our actions we can make this world a better place. Amen.

Anna Cloeter

A Promise of God

Read: Romans 8:28

Think about how much time you spend worrying about uncertainties. It can get pretty stressful thinking about all those tests, relationship problems, and college options. In Romans 8:28, we find relief.

There are two parts to this passage. First, Paul says, "And we know that for those who love God . . ." Think about this for a moment. It is a promise. It says "And we *know*," meaning it is a fact, something that we do not doubt. Christ wants our lives to be filled with joy and happiness. He is working in your life right now for your good, even if you cannot understand how. With this also comes reassurance. We do not have to carry the weight of the world on our shoulders. We can relax and have confidence that God has control over all things.

Paul concludes his thought by saying, "for those who are called according to His purpose." God has a purpose for all of His children. Even before you were born, your heavenly Father had blessings to give you, and He continues to invite you to experience these in your everyday life. God has a great plan and purpose for each of His children, and with this reassurance, we do not have to be afraid of anything.

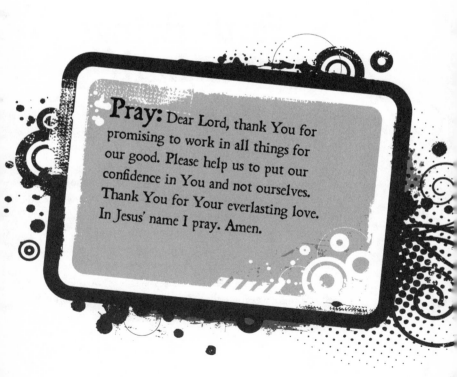

Pray: Dear Lord, thank You for promising to work in all things for our good. Please help us to put our confidence in You and not ourselves. Thank You for Your everlasting love. In Jesus' name I pray. Amen.

Jacob Mayer

Faith Brings Strength

Read: Psalm 34:17

Ever since I learned what destruction tornadoes could produce, I have been nervous when a bad storm develops and even more scared when a tornado warning is issued for my county. Recently, some severe storms blew through my corner of the world. It was a Saturday night, and my parents and I had gone an hour away from home to be with my aunt and uncle for a trivia night. We had left my sisters at home for the evening because there was not enough room on the team for all of us to play. Just as we walked in the door, we got a call telling us about the strength of the storms coming toward our home. We had a decision to make. We were not sure what to do. We decided to get home. So we drove the hour to return home. We were just in time. Within thirty minutes, the first of many tornado-infested storms entered our county. One tornado was apparently headed directly for our street.

As I sat in the basement, I prayed that God would protect us when the storm hit. The power went out immediately and was out for the rest of the night. The last weather report on television showed a bright red and pink mass directly over us. The radio was also dead, so the only information we could get was from relatives and friends calling our cell phone.

Amazingly, the next information we received was that the brunt of the storm had gone about five miles south of us. While I had been praying, a calm feeling had come over me. Those prayers were definitely rough around the edges, but God does not need us to say certain words or phrases. As it says in Psalm 34:17, "When the righteous cry for help, the LORD hears and delivers them out of all their troubles."

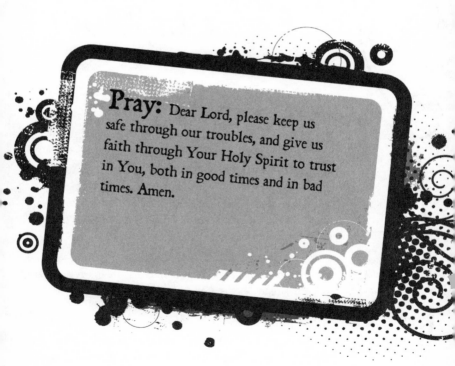

Pray: Dear Lord, please keep us safe through our troubles, and give us faith through Your Holy Spirit to trust in You, both in good times and in bad times. Amen.

Krista Wegener

Leper or Not

Read: Mark 1:40–45

Why is it that a carpenter's house is the one that needs the most repairs? Or a landscaper's yard is full of weeds? At the end of a hard day's work, those people want to relax. You would think that professionals would apply their skills to their home lives, but even though they have the ability, they are not always willing. In Mark 1:40–45, Jesus shows His willingness to heal a man of leprosy.

Jesus has the power to make a difference in our lives, and more important, He loves us. So besides having the power, Jesus has the desire to help us. Consider the leper as he came to Jesus while He was preaching. As you can imagine, there was a huge crowd of people. This man, with festering sores all over his body, walks through this crowd of people to get to Jesus. Instead of remaining in seclusion, away from the general population, this man boldly approaches Christ.

Leprosy is a chronic disease with sores that enlarge and spread, accompanied by deformities and mutilations. It's possible that the crowd may have spit at him, ridiculed him, and been generally pretty nasty to him, but he did not let that stop him.

He knew he needed healing, and he was determined to get it. Once he got to Jesus, verse 41 tells us, "Moved with pity, [Jesus] stretched out His hand and touched him." He touched the man! The leper! Jesus reached out and touched an unclean man. He could have just said, "Be healed," and it would have been done. He had done it before. But this time He touched the sick man. Why? To show the man that He cared about him.

We can take comfort in the knowledge that Jesus cares about us too! Whether we win or lose, are ugly or attractive, Jesus loves us. He is with us all the time, healing us in our family life, in our schoolwork, and in everything we do. He wants us to see that in every situation there is hope because He is with us.

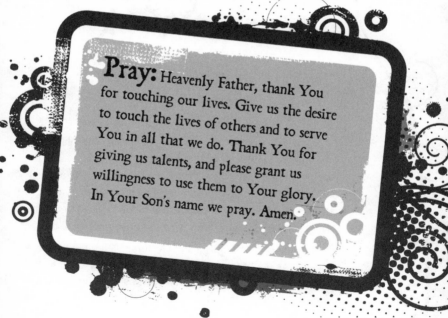

Pray: Heavenly Father, thank You for touching our lives. Give us the desire to touch the lives of others and to serve You in all that we do. Thank You for giving us talents, and please grant us willingness to use them to Your glory. In Your Son's name we pray. Amen.

Liz Peterson

Hope for the Weak

Read: 2 Timothy 2:13

How frequently are you so bombarded with obligations and emotions of this world that even your faith seems weak? This happens all too often in my life, and I find myself feeling guilty and alone. In 2 Timothy, however, we are told that even when we are weak, God is not. God remains faithful even when we cannot. It also says that He will always carry out His promises to us.

There are stories throughout history about those who were sick, and God let them die. And there are stories of those who were hurting, and God did not take away their pain. Too often, we want God to do things our way and in our time, but that is not faithfulness. That is magic.

God promises to be faithful, which means He promises never to leave us. Faithfulness is not God ensuring our popularity, good health, or wealth. Instead, God assures us of His continual presence in our lives. When your friend was sick, God was there. When you were hurting, God was there too. Whether or not we can sense it, no matter the circumstances, we can rest assured that God is with us as a trusted Friend and loving Father. When this earthly life ends, He will take us home to live with Him forever.

Take comfort in 2 Timothy 2:13. When you are too weak even to bow your head to Jesus Christ, He is right there, forever, fulfilling His promises.

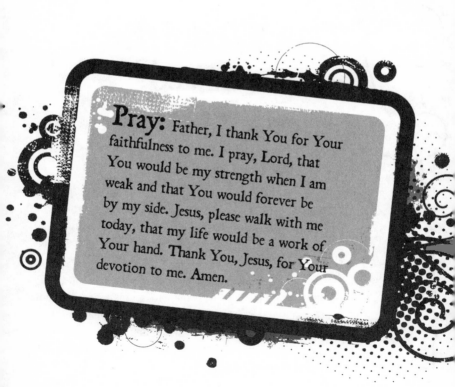

Pray: Father, I thank You for Your faithfulness to me. I pray, Lord, that You would be my strength when I am weak and that You would forever be by my side. Jesus, please walk with me today, that my life would be a work of Your hand. Thank You, Jesus, for Your devotion to me. Amen.

Heather Nagel

Will I Be Saved?

Read: Mark 16:16

Will I be saved? A lot of people ask that question. Maybe they have done some things in their lives of which God disapproves. Maybe at some point they turned away from God. There are many things that can make people unsure of their salvation.

I had a friend who questioned her salvation. She had a rough past, got involved with the wrong group, and did some questionable things. She did not put much emphasis on God. Later, she realized she was doing something wrong and returned to God. She left her past behind, but she still has that doubt in her mind as to whether or not she will be saved. She believes in God, but she does not know if God will save her because of her past. However, Mark 16:16 says, "Whoever believes and is baptized will be saved." So, will she be saved? Thanks be to God that that question need not be asked, because, as the Gospel promises, we will be saved by grace through faith in Christ Jesus.

Pray: Dear Lord, thank You for Your reassurance of our salvation. Help us to teach others the goodness of Your love. In Your name we pray. Amen.

Cody Deaton

The Atoning Sacrifice

Read: 1 John 2:2

Mark was a boy who never got into trouble. He always did his homework on time, listened to his parents, and obeyed his teachers—until one day Billy and Joe moved onto Mark's street a few weeks after school was out for the summer. Mark could tell that they were a little different, but he went ahead and introduced himself to them, and they all became friends.

One day while they were strolling around the neighborhood, Billy and Joe spotted a house they presumed to be vacant and began busting out the windows. Mark ran up to them shouting, "Stop! Stop!" because he knew that it was Mr. Dell's house. Billy and Joe heard the door open, so they ran away, leaving Mark there to face Mr. Dell. Mr. Dell had evidently already called the police, because the sheriff was coming down the street. Mark took responsibility for the other two boys and paid to repair the windows himself. He also apologized to Mr. Dell.

In this story, we are like Billy and Joe. We commit sins, but we do not usually take responsibility for those sins. Billy and Joe were strong enough to commit the crime, but when it came time to take responsibility for their actions, they ran in fear, just as we do when we are faced with our sins. Thanks to Jesus, we do not have to run anymore!

Mark made the redeeming sacrifice in this story. Mark, the boy who did not throw a single stone and who even tried to stop the other boys, took the fall for everyone. Mark was to Billy and Joe as Jesus Christ is to us. We, as Christians, disobey God's Law constantly. But Jesus kept it perfectly in our place. He never slipped up or made a mistake. He was perfect and strong enough to stand up and take the punishment for the people He loved and cared for, becoming the atoning sacrifice for our sins. Thanks to Jesus, we do not receive the punishment we deserve.

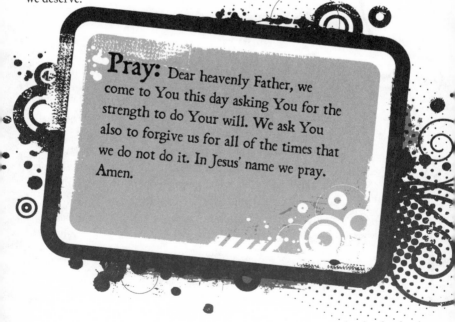

Pray: Dear heavenly Father, we come to You this day asking You for the strength to do Your will. We ask You also to forgive us for all of the times that we do not do it. In Jesus' name we pray. Amen.

Abby Newman

The Perfect Plan

Read: Jeremiah 29:11

Do you ever feel like you are out of control and nothing is going as you planned? Well, in this verse, God lets us know that He has a plan for us, and He will not let us down. Sometimes we do not know what we should be doing in life. If we move to a new school or a new state or country, when tragic events happen, or when things seem to be spinning out of control, God lets us know that He has a plan for us. And He never fails. As it says in Jeremiah, these plans are to "prosper" us and "not to harm" us (NIV). God would never do anything to harm us. Even if bad things happen and we wonder why God lets them happen, it is not because He wants to hurt us. We almost never know why bad things happen, but we do know that God promises to cause good to come out of these things. You can trust the Lord and have faith in Him. Just put everything into His hands and let it go, knowing

He will take care of it.

It also says in this verse that His plans are to give us "hope and a future" (NIV). God knows our needs and our wants, and He will surely provide. Our future is in His hands. What better person could you have picked for the job? We simply need to remember that we do not have to worry because God is in control of all things.

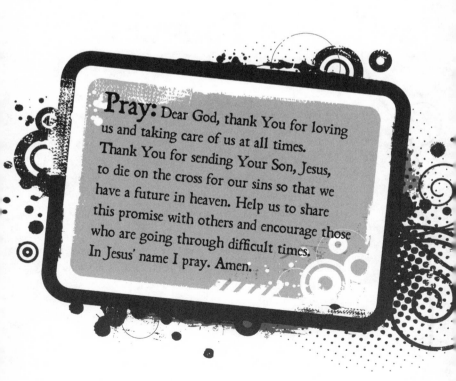

Pray: Dear God, thank You for loving us and taking care of us at all times. Thank You for sending Your Son, Jesus, to die on the cross for our sins so that we have a future in heaven. Help us to share this promise with others and encourage those who are going through difficult times. In Jesus' name I pray. Amen.

Shalimar Davis

Tongues

Read: James 3:9–10

This Bible verse happens to be one of my favorites because it can be helpful to all people. Every day people use their tongues, whether for talking, eating, or just sticking it out at other people. In science class, we are taught how much our tongues do for us. This Bible verse makes you think: how much good actually comes from the tongue?

How many people can boast that they have not said anything bad about someone else? It is scary to think that the same tongue with which you curse others and swear, you also talk to God. When I read this verse and analyze it, I find the thought of my tongue being used for these two very different things profound! God has given us His Word to direct us. These verses remind us to use the gifts God has given us to honor Him.

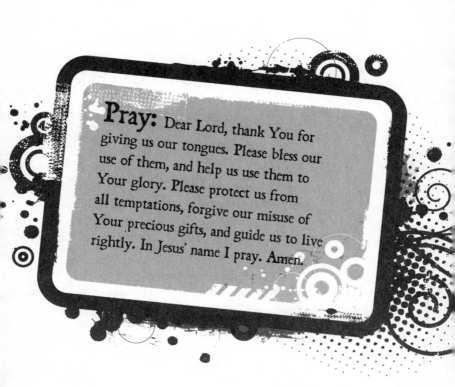

Pray: Dear Lord, thank You for giving us our tongues. Please bless our use of them, and help us use them to Your glory. Please protect us from all temptations, forgive our misuse of Your precious gifts, and guide us to live rightly. In Jesus' name I pray. Amen.

Ryan Permison

Leaning on God's Strength

Read: Philippians 4:13

In our lives we all have problems, whether with a friend, a co-worker, or a family member. We all struggle. There is not one person on this earth who does not have problems. But no matter what happens, your Savior will always be there to pick you up when you are down.

For example, the loss of a family member can be hard for anyone. In those times, remember His promises to love and care for you. As He said in Hebrews 13:5, "I will never leave you nor forsake you." Whatever troubles you are going through right now, know that God will give you peace in the midst of these storms.

Whatever the problem, your heavenly Father will listen to you. He wants you to tell Him what is on your mind.

God knows you inside and out, so when you talk to Him, you are talking to a very close friend. Whatever has happened, wherever you are, remember that God is always there to guide, bless, and comfort you now and forever.

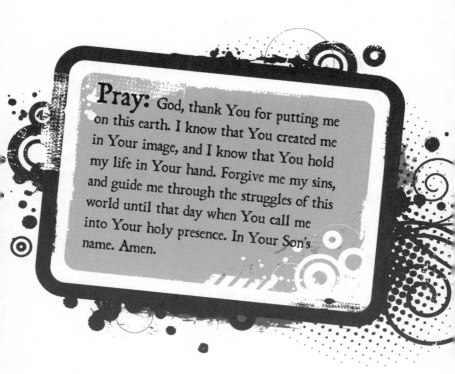

Pray: God, thank You for putting me on this earth. I know that You created me in Your image, and I know that You hold my life in Your hand. Forgive me my sins, and guide me through the struggles of this world until that day when You call me into Your holy presence. In Your Son's name. Amen.

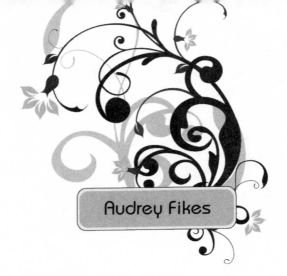

Audrey Fikes

Prayerfulness

Read: Ephesians 6:18

This verse tells us that we should pray to God no matter the circumstances. Do not just pray when things are going poorly or when you want to ask for something. Pray when things are going well, and be thankful for all you have. Do not forget to pray for others.

Try to remember that your prayers should not be selfish. It is not wrong to pray for things that you want, but it is good to focus on things that you, your family, your friends, or even strangers need. When you pray, remember that God will always answer. It may not be the answer you want, but He will answer. Finally, remember that no matter how good or bad things are, there is no problem so big that God cannot handle it and no worry too small that God doesn't care.

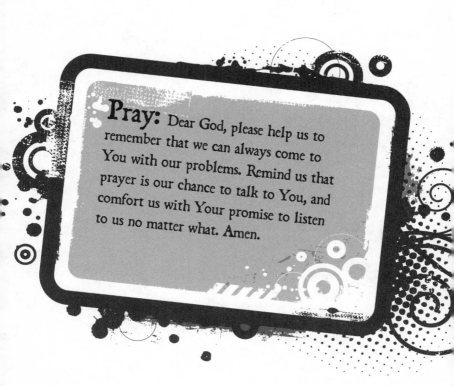

Pray: Dear God, please help us to remember that we can always come to You with our problems. Remind us that prayer is our chance to talk to You, and comfort us with Your promise to listen to us no matter what. Amen.

When the
righteous thrive,
the people rejoice.
Proverbs 29:2 (NIV)

Miranda Jackson

Defeating Death

Read: Romans 6:9

Andrew is scared. In fact, he's terrified. Terrified of the treatments, terrified of living this way, and most of all, terrified of dying. The doctors estimate that he has only a couple of months to live. Andrew has cancer.

Death has been the only thing Andrew can think about lately. He is only eleven years old, and even though he knows the story of Christ's sacrifice for him, he finds it hard to find comfort in it. It frightens him to think of the number of sins he has committed throughout his life.

However, Andrew's pastor has been visiting him regularly while he's in the hospital. Through God's Word, the Holy Spirit is instilling a remarkable faith in Andrew. The Spirit is showing Andrew that his sins are completely washed away by Christ's death on the cross. Because of this, Andrew has been able to find comfort in the words of the Bible. Romans 6:9 has made Andrew realize that because his Lord and Savior conquered death, he will do the same. Andrew now understands that a mortal death is not the end of his life, and he looks forward to the life he will live in heaven.

Like Andrew, we as Christians realize the significance of Christ's sacrifice for our sins. No amount of good works on our part could ever come close to making us worthy of the gift we are given through Christ's death and resurrection. The words of our verse allow us to be certain that our Lord conquered death. Death no longer has mastery over Him or us. We do not have to be afraid of dying. Heaven is a great reward, and Jesus won it for us. We can rejoice in His death and resurrection and know that as we get nearer to our own death, we are even closer to meeting our Lord face-to-face. What an amazing blessing!

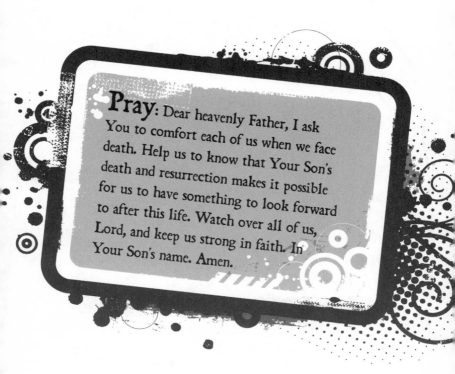

Pray: Dear heavenly Father, I ask You to comfort each of us when we face death. Help us to know that Your Son's death and resurrection makes it possible for us to have something to look forward to after this life. Watch over all of us, Lord, and keep us strong in faith. In Your Son's name. Amen.

Candice Noelker

Out of Jail

Read: 1 John 4:9–10

Pretend for a minute that you have been arrested. You are sentenced to life in prison without chance of parole. One day, someone sends in his son and tells you his son is to take your place in jail and you are to be released forever. You do not know this man, let alone love him. But he obviously loves you very much, enough to give up his own son for you.

We don't have to pretend. We were in jail and deserved to stay there forever. We were imprisoned for our wrongdoing, and there was nothing we could do about it.

But God does not leave us sitting in jail. He sent His one and only Son into the world, our jail, to save us from our sins. God did not save us because of our love for Him. God loves us so much that He sent Jesus to die for us before we knew Him, much less loved Him. Jesus Christ became the atoning sacrifice for our sins. Jesus has served our prison sentence for us. Thanks be to God that we now live with Him in freedom and in the blessed assurance of eternal life!

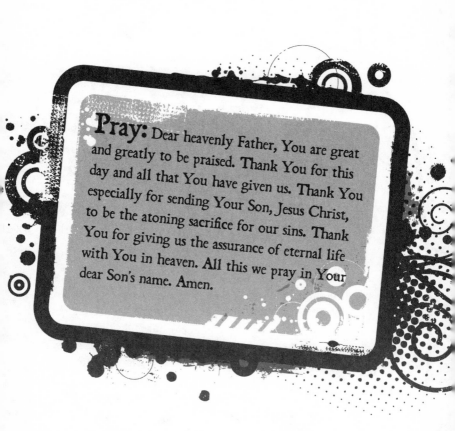

Pray: Dear heavenly Father, You are great and greatly to be praised. Thank You for this day and all that You have given us. Thank You especially for sending Your Son, Jesus Christ, to be the atoning sacrifice for our sins. Thank You for giving us the assurance of eternal life with You in heaven. All this we pray in Your dear Son's name. Amen.

Anonymous

Apparel for the Unloving and Uncompassionate

Read: Colossians 3:12–14

In a world where violence is commonplace, suffering is ordinary, and love and compassion are rare, it is easy to become calloused and accustomed to the horrors going on around us. We are bombarded with so many things that we try not to get too emotional, or not to care, because ultimately it is not our problem. Many today simply ask, "Why should I care?"

We should care because Jesus cared. He had compassion on those who were less fortunate than He, on all those around Him who were hurting and broken. Peeking out from our comfortable world and viewing the devastation, brokenness, and evil brutality that the world dishes out can be depressing and disheartening. However, if we, each one of us, person by person, show compassion and love, Jesus can use us to heal a little bit of brokenness in our world.

God knows it is impossible as human beings to be as intentionally loving and compassionate as He is, and that is why Paul instructs us to clothe ourselves with love, compassion, humility, and all the other admirable traits mentioned in our reading from Colossians. The spectacular thing is we do not have to travel around the world to find this brand-name clothing line! We can just ask God to give us His love and compassion, and He does so for free!

As we clothe ourselves in His love and compassion, we will begin to notice the needs of people in our everyday lives, whether it be at school, work, or in our community. Through the power of the Holy Spirit, we will want to reach out to them, love them, and care for them. By saying a prayer, sharing a smile, giving a hug, or encouraging someone in need of love, Christ can heal their brokenness through us. In addition to the blessing we will be to others, the Body of Christ will be strengthened through the love and compassion we have toward one another.

The next time you feel tempted to bury your head in the sand to tune out the tragedies happening in our world, think about how Christ has clothed us with His perfect love, and let that love radically change your life.

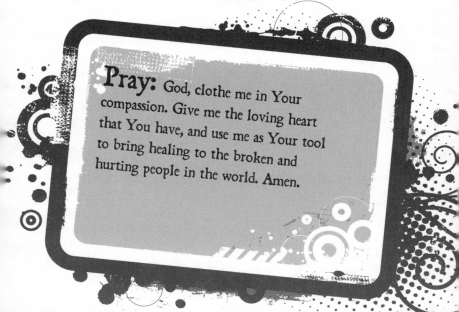

Pray: God, clothe me in Your compassion. Give me the loving heart that You have, and use me as Your tool to bring healing to the broken and hurting people in the world. Amen.

Amy Dowdle

Perseverance

Read: James 1:2–4

James is a good book to read when you are facing hard times. This passage tells us that when we go through tough times, we must persevere and never give up. In order for us truly to come out of a bad situation and learn something from it, we have to allow ourselves to go through it. We all go through times in our lives when it seems like we cannot make it through another day, but Christ is always with us.

God does not allow us to face more than we can handle, and He has promised to bless us in all things. It may seem like what you are facing now is too hard, but with God by your side and God's Word to guide you, you will make it. Even though the situation looks like nothing good will come out of it, something will. Therefore, you can always find peace in the Lord. Take time each day to read and reflect on the Word. After you meditate on the Word, take time to pray and thank God. Tell Him the worries of your heart, and ask Him to help you persevere when it seems that you cannot make it. He will always listen and answer you.

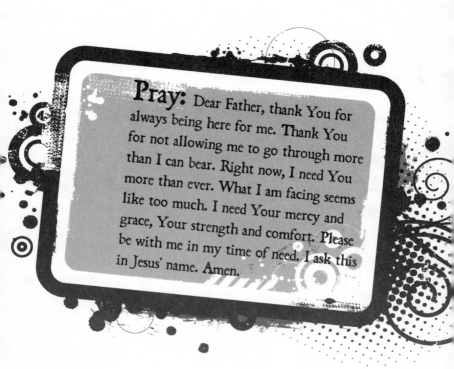

Pray: Dear Father, thank You for always being here for me. Thank You for not allowing me to go through more than I can bear. Right now, I need You more than ever. What I am facing seems like too much. I need Your mercy and grace, Your strength and comfort. Please be with me in my time of need. I ask this in Jesus' name. Amen.

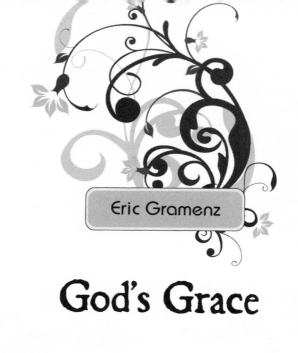

Eric Gramenz

God's Grace

Read: Romans 8:1–2

We are all constantly under the law. We are under town laws and state and federal laws. If we break any of these laws, we are subject to the punishment of the government. Most important, we are under God's Law. If we break God's Law, we are worthy of being sent to hell, and because we all have sinned, that is what we deserve.

God, however, did not want that to happen. He sent His Son, Jesus Christ, to take away our sins. Jesus came to earth as someone under the Law, even though He was above it because it was God who gave the Law. He then took our sins on Himself and died under the Law, even though He was sinless and without defect. By suffering for our sins as though they were His own, He made us perfect in the eyes of God. Now, even though we sin, we know that if we believe in Christ we are forgiven. We will go to heaven, not because of anything we did, but because of what Christ did.

We know that Christ has delivered us from the condemnation of the Law. This doesn't mean we can go out and sin all we want. Rather, because of our new life in Christ, we seek to obey His Law and follow His Commandments.

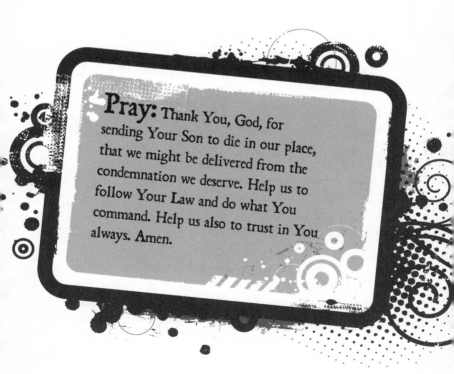

Pray: Thank You, God, for sending Your Son to die in our place, that we might be delivered from the condemnation we deserve. Help us to follow Your Law and do what You command. Help us also to trust in You always. Amen.

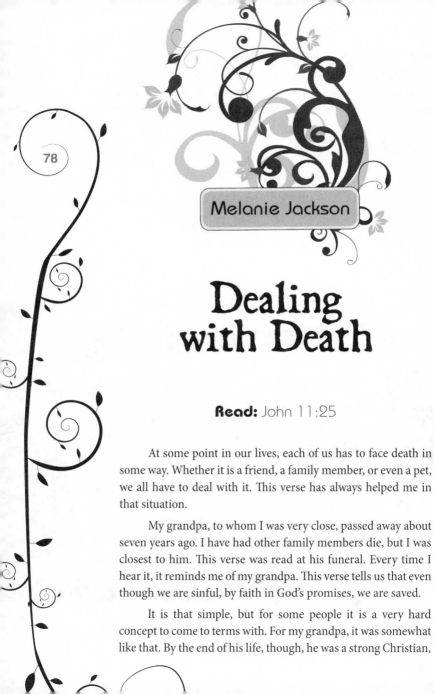

Melanie Jackson

Dealing with Death

Read: John 11:25

At some point in our lives, each of us has to face death in some way. Whether it is a friend, a family member, or even a pet, we all have to deal with it. This verse has always helped me in that situation.

My grandpa, to whom I was very close, passed away about seven years ago. I have had other family members die, but I was closest to him. This verse was read at his funeral. Every time I hear it, it reminds me of my grandpa. This verse tells us that even though we are sinful, by faith in God's promises, we are saved.

It is that simple, but for some people it is a very hard concept to come to terms with. For my grandpa, it was somewhat like that. By the end of his life, though, he was a strong Christian, and it showed through his actions and words. He knew that because of faith, he would have eternal life with Christ.

In our verse, Jesus promises, "Whoever believes in Me, though he die, yet shall he live." This is the Good News of Jesus Christ: even though we are sinful and die, we will live forever with our Lord Jesus Christ in heaven. Death no longer has mastery over us, and we can be thankful, knowing that our loved ones who have gone before us and we ourselves will be together one day with Christ, living eternally in heaven.

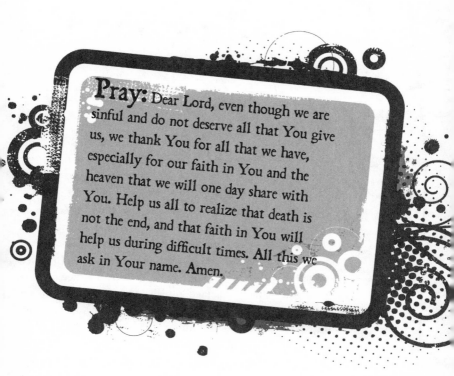

Pray: Dear Lord, even though we are sinful and do not deserve all that You give us, we thank You for all that we have, especially for our faith in You and the heaven that we will one day share with You. Help us all to realize that death is not the end, and that faith in You will help us during difficult times. All this we ask in Your name. Amen.

Elisabeth
Shearier

Falling Short

Read: Romans 3:23–24

In middle school, my friends and I loved to play on the monkey bars. We would jump from the platform and try to grab hold of the round metal bars. Very rarely would we succeed. One day, my friend Alyssa decided to take a running start, grab the bar, and pull herself up. My friends and I pulled ourselves up onto the monkey bars and got comfortable to watch her perform this great act. She walked back a few feet and then started running. She reached the edge of the platform and jumped. However, her jump was not quite long enough, and she smacked into the ground face-first. She landed in such a way that she pinned her arm underneath her and broke it. She had to be carried back into the school building by my fifth-grade teacher.

Like Alyssa, we, too, fall short. We cannot get to heaven on our own. Relying on our own strength, we will always fall short of God. Romans 3:23 says, "For all have sinned and fall short of the glory of God." Because we are sinners, we cannot come to faith on our own and be saved. However, the good news is that Paul continues in verse 24 to say, "and are justified by His grace as a gift, through the redemption that is in Christ Jesus." God loves us so much that He picks us up after we fall, just as my teacher picked up Alyssa and carried her inside. Through the work of His Son, Jesus Christ, God picks us up and carries us to be with Him in heaven.

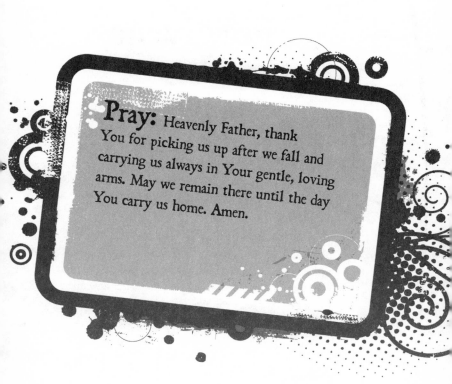

Pray: Heavenly Father, thank You for picking us up after we fall and carrying us always in Your gentle, loving arms. May we remain there until the day You carry us home. Amen.

Paul Canales

Forgiveness

Read: Matthew 18:21–35

Have you ever had someone do something so bad to you that you were not sure if you would ever get over it? Odds are you probably got over it a lot faster than you thought you would. You forgave the person for what he or she did, and now things are going well again.

In this Bible passage, Peter asks Jesus how many times to forgive someone. Jesus responds by telling him seventy times seven. Jesus was basically saying that you need to forgive people every time they wrong you. No matter how many times it happens, you need to forgive.

The love of our heavenly Father is what saved us from paying the price for our sin. He forgave us our transgressions and removed our iniquities. In the same way, we can forgive those who sin against us.

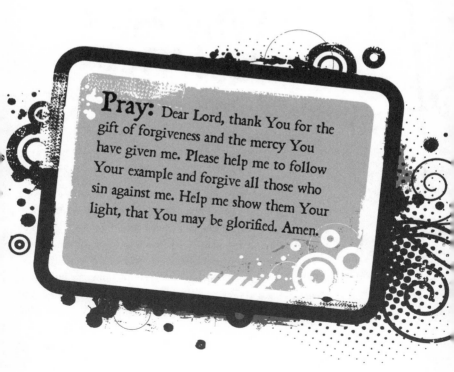

Pray: Dear Lord, thank You for the gift of forgiveness and the mercy You have given me. Please help me to follow Your example and forgive all those who sin against me. Help me show them Your light, that You may be glorified. Amen.

Katie Rieckers

Why Am I like This?

Read: 1 Corinthians 13:12

Have you ever woken up one morning and looked in the mirror thinking, Man, I look hideous today? I imagine everyone has done it at least once or twice. Many people think that they have to look a certain way and that being different is bad. For example, look at the world's obsession with being thin. There is so much pressure on young people to be cool and attractive. Many teens, and even younger kids, come home crying, telling their parents that they hate the way they look because they were teased today for being a littler bigger, a little shorter, a little taller, and on and on.

In 1 Samuel 16:7, God tells us, "Man looks on the outward appearance, but the LORD looks on the heart." Some people who read this verse say, "Okay. God said that He looks at our hearts and not at our appearances, but does that mean that we are still ugly?" Absolutely not! The Bible says in Genesis 1:27, "So God created man in His own image, in the image of God He created him; male and female He created them." How wonderful to know that we are created in the image of God and that He has blessed us with the gift of being different.

We may not look the way we want to, and we certainly do not look perfect. But God also tells us that one day we will be perfect, inside and out! Can you imagine? God will make everything beautiful, including us! Then we will not look in a mirror and say, "Oh, my, look at me." Instead, we will forever be singing praises to God and continually praising His name for making us exactly who we are!

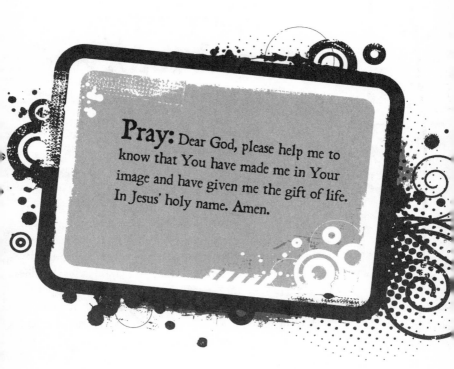

Pray: Dear God, please help me to know that You have made me in Your image and have given me the gift of life. In Jesus' holy name. Amen.

Kurt McKenna

Running for Victory

Read: 1 Corinthians 9:24

When I was in elementary school, there was an annual track meet between all of the Christians schools of the same association. Months beforehand, during PE, we would train and train and train. All of my classmates and I would train for our events: the running long jump, the high jump, the 50-yard dash, the 4 × 4 relay, and the mile. We were so excited when the day of the meet came. Personally, I loved the 50-yard dash. I was the best. When my event came up, I thought I would surely win. They called us to take our marks. "Go!" We were off. I was leading, pushing my hardest. When it was over, the results showed that I finished in second place.

"Do you not know that in a race all the runners run, but only one receives the prize? So run that you may obtain it" (1 Corinthians 9:24). Paul tells us that everyone who runs in the race trains for it. They run, not to finish last or even in second place, but to win. That goal, that achievement, is what they run for. In this life, we live for God because of all that He has done for us through His Son, Jesus Christ. Therefore, let us live a life that is worthy of His holy name.

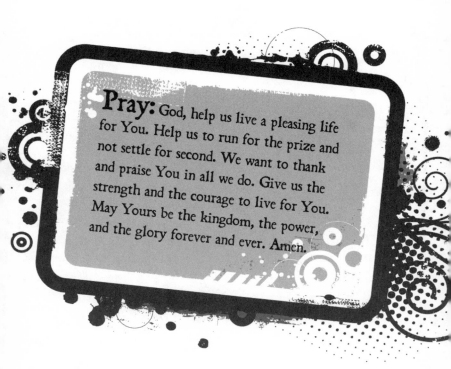

Pray: God, help us live a pleasing life for You. Help us to run for the prize and not settle for second. We want to thank and praise You in all we do. Give us the strength and the courage to live for You. May Yours be the kingdom, the power, and the glory forever and ever. Amen.

Karina Heredia

True Love

Read: 1 Corinthians 13:4–7

What people call "love" is not always seen the way it is described in these verses. In fact, it rarely is shown this way because of the world in which we live. The love described by St. Paul is actually the love God has for us and is an example for all of us as to how we should love and expect to be loved.

God's love for us is strong and unconditional. His love for us is so strong that He sent His only Son to die for our sins. God has loved us despite the sins we have committed and will keep loving us until the end of time. This love is one of a kind.

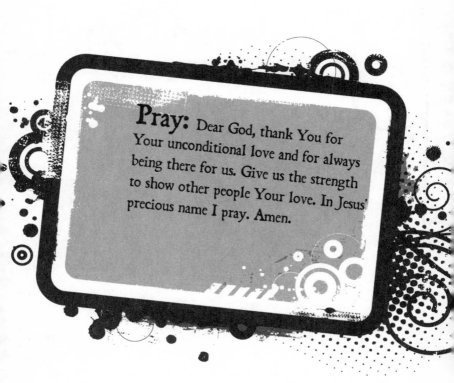

Pray: Dear God, thank You for Your unconditional love and for always being there for us. Give us the strength to show other people Your love. In Jesus' precious name I pray. Amen.

89

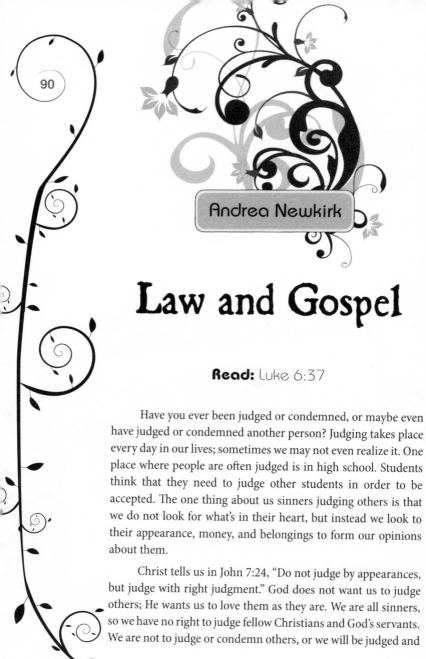

Andrea Newkirk

Law and Gospel

Read: Luke 6:37

Have you ever been judged or condemned, or maybe even have judged or condemned another person? Judging takes place every day in our lives; sometimes we may not even realize it. One place where people are often judged is in high school. Students think that they need to judge other students in order to be accepted. The one thing about us sinners judging others is that we do not look for what's in their heart, but instead we look to their appearance, money, and belongings to form our opinions about them.

Christ tells us in John 7:24, "Do not judge by appearances, but judge with right judgment." God does not want us to judge others; He wants us to love them as they are. We are all sinners, so we have no right to judge fellow Christians and God's servants. We are not to judge or condemn others, or we will be judged and condemned. Jesus reminds us that the spirit of judgment with which we treat others will also be the spirit of judgment that may be used to judge us. Instead, we are to forgive those who have done us wrong, just as Christ forgives us.

Christ has died for us; therefore, we have received the gift of eternal life and are forgiven. And we have the promise from Romans 8:1, "There is therefore now no condemnation for those who are in Christ Jesus."

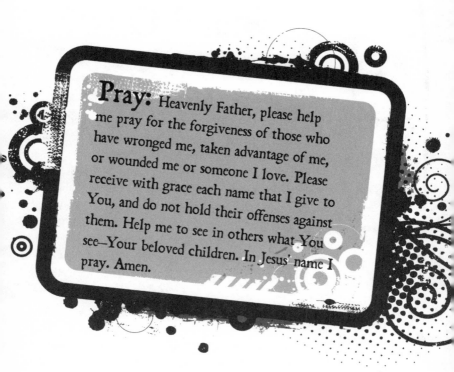

Pray: Heavenly Father, please help me pray for the forgiveness of those who have wronged me, taken advantage of me, or wounded me or someone I love. Please receive with grace each name that I give to You, and do not hold their offenses against them. Help me to see in others what You see—Your beloved children. In Jesus' name I pray. Amen.

Mikaela Barz

Stand Out

Read: 1 Thessalonians 5:15

This is a difficult verse to follow. According to our sinful nature, we feel that it is our right to get revenge if somebody hurts us. But God does not want us to return hate with hate, but rather to return hate with love. We are told to turn the other cheek (Matthew 5:39) and pray for those who persecute us (Matthew 5:44). God wants us to treat our enemies in such a way that they notice that there's something different about the way we act. Not only should our enemies wonder what's different about us, but also our friends. They, too, should be able to see Christ through our actions.

Having your friends notice your faith does not mean that you have to carry a Bible everywhere or wear T-shirts with Christian themes every day. Your friends should notice the difference in you by the way you act. Go out of your way to be kind to people, especially those who are sometimes forgotten or rejected by others. When you truly care about others, they will see Christ's love in you.

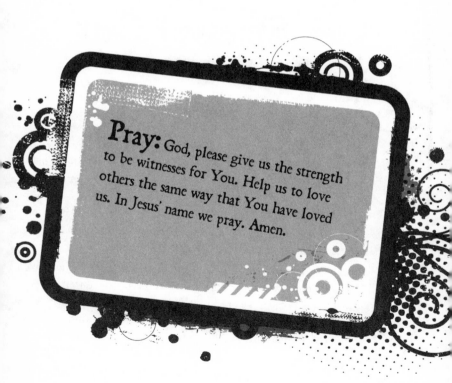

Pray: God, please give us the strength to be witnesses for You. Help us to love others the same way that You have loved us. In Jesus' name we pray. Amen.

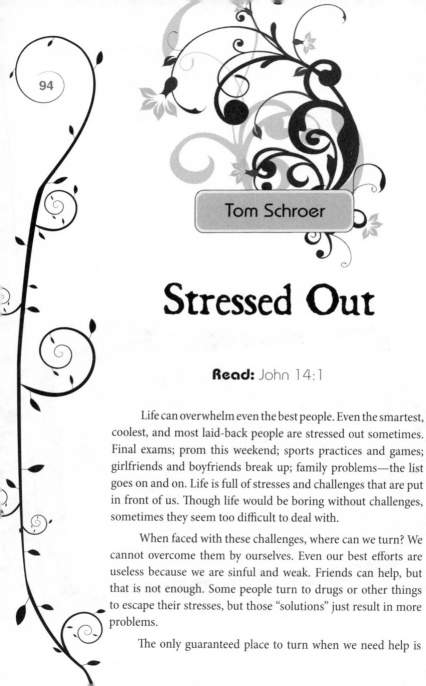

Tom Schroer

Stressed Out

Read: John 14:1

Life can overwhelm even the best people. Even the smartest, coolest, and most laid-back people are stressed out sometimes. Final exams; prom this weekend; sports practices and games; girlfriends and boyfriends break up; family problems—the list goes on and on. Life is full of stresses and challenges that are put in front of us. Though life would be boring without challenges, sometimes they seem too difficult to deal with.

When faced with these challenges, where can we turn? We cannot overcome them by ourselves. Even our best efforts are useless because we are sinful and weak. Friends can help, but that is not enough. Some people turn to drugs or other things to escape their stresses, but those "solutions" just result in more problems.

The only guaranteed place to turn when we need help is

our heavenly Father. God's Word reminds us to trust in the Father, who with Jesus and the Holy Spirit is true God. The Lord will give us strength to overcome our challenges. When all seems hopeless, He gives us the gift of eternal life. Jesus went through everything that we have gone through. He promises not to give us more than we can handle. We can put our trust in Him because He has been there too.

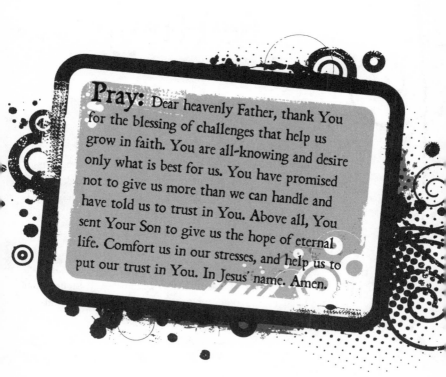

Pray: Dear heavenly Father, thank You for the blessing of challenges that help us grow in faith. You are all-knowing and desire only what is best for us. You have promised not to give us more than we can handle and have told us to trust in You. Above all, You sent Your Son to give us the hope of eternal life. Comfort us in our stresses, and help us to put our trust in You. In Jesus' name. Amen.

Samantha Flores

Be Happy!

Read: Psalm 126

Sometimes we have bad days, and sometimes we have really good days. On the days we struggle, we may be at a loss as to what to do. We often want to push God aside and take control of the situation ourselves. We soon realize that without God's help, we cannot win. We just can't.

Our God is great and blesses us. He comes through for us, just as He did with His people in Psalm 126. The captives of Zion were praising the Lord and were thankful for what He had done for them. There is much rejoicing, because even though they were having some rough times, they remembered all the ways in which God had blessed them.

Even when you are going through trials, you can, with the power of the Holy Spirit, keep your focus on God and His Word, which will get you through.

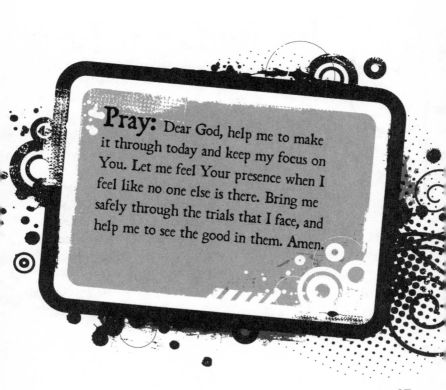

Pray: Dear God, help me to make it through today and keep my focus on You. Let me feel Your presence when I feel like no one else is there. Bring me safely through the trials that I face, and help me to see the good in them. Amen.

Eric Schepman

Insignificant Loss

Read: Psalm 73:26

As a junior in high school, I remember playing in a basketball game that I really believed we could win. Our season started kind of slow with some close losses that dampened our confidence. Going into the game against the Hornets, we really believed we would come out on top. Before the game, our coach gave us a pep talk to fire us up and to build our confidence even more. After our team prayer, we ran out on the court, believing we were the better team. As the game went on, we slowly fell behind. The Hornets were getting to all the loose balls and were just better athletes than we were. After the game, we sat in the locker room, disappointed over the loss.

Coach told us to learn from the loss and to forget about the agony of defeat. He reminded us that it was only a game. We truly needed to focus on the fact that even though we may not be talented enough or athletic enough to win a game like this, God is the true rock and strength of our lives. We can take comfort in knowing that disappointments in our lives are insignificant compared to what God has promised us—eternal life forever in heaven with Him.

Whether it is a basketball game or a breakup with a boyfriend or girlfriend, God will always be with us, even when we feel alone or without hope. We have the hope of eternal life! "I count everything as loss because of the surpassing worth of knowing Christ Jesus my Lord" (Philippians 3:8).

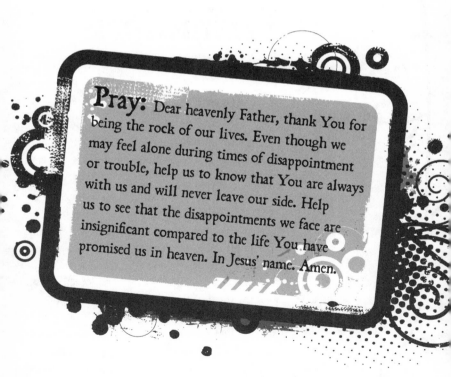

Pray: Dear heavenly Father, thank You for being the rock of our lives. Even though we may feel alone during times of disappointment or trouble, help us to know that You are always with us and will never leave our side. Help us to see that the disappointments we face are insignificant compared to the life You have promised us in heaven. In Jesus' name. Amen.

Emilie Rupp

Faithfulness

Read: Psalm 63:8

All people try to be faithful to someone, whether family, friends, boyfriends, or girlfriends. But what about God? How often do we remember to be eternally faithful to Him?

Unfortunately, we are not always faithful to God. Yet He continues to do so much for us and to be faithful to us. He gave us His Son to save our souls. He gives us food, clothing, and shelter to care for our bodies, and He continues to love us with His perfect love. We may be thankful, at least for a little while, but then, too often, we blow it all off and forget He ever did anything for us. The only thanks He really wants from us is to love Him and believe His promises. Unfortunately, sometimes we refuse to do even that.

Yet even when we are unfaithful and forget His promises, God remains faithful to us. He keeps His promises and blesses us in every way.

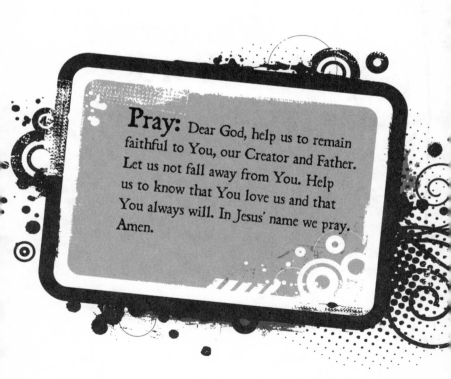

Pray: Dear God, help us to remain faithful to You, our Creator and Father. Let us not fall away from You. Help us to know that You love us and that You always will. In Jesus' name we pray. Amen.

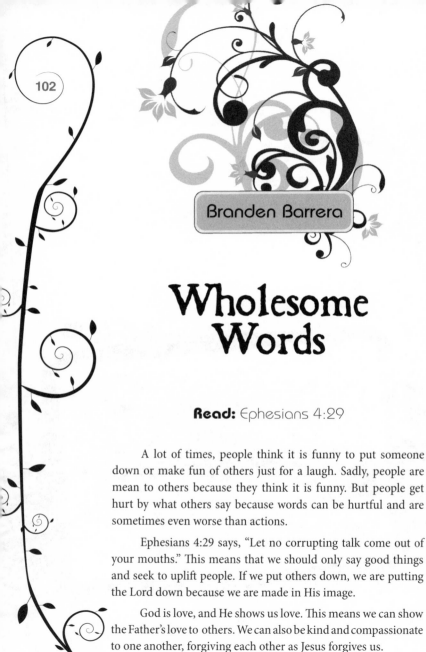

Branden Barrera

Wholesome Words

Read: Ephesians 4:29

A lot of times, people think it is funny to put someone down or make fun of others just for a laugh. Sadly, people are mean to others because they think it is funny. But people get hurt by what others say because words can be hurtful and are sometimes even worse than actions.

Ephesians 4:29 says, "Let no corrupting talk come out of your mouths." This means that we should only say good things and seek to uplift people. If we put others down, we are putting the Lord down because we are made in His image.

God is love, and He shows us love. This means we can show the Father's love to others. We can also be kind and compassionate to one another, forgiving each other as Jesus forgives us.

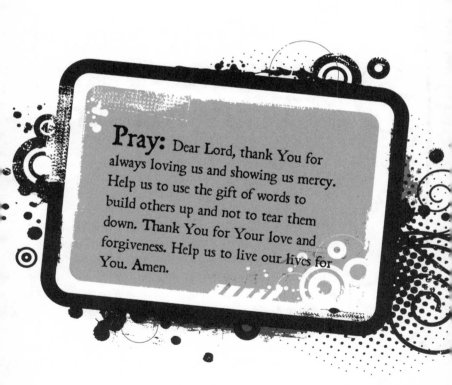

Pray: Dear Lord, thank You for always loving us and showing us mercy. Help us to use the gift of words to build others up and not to tear them down. Thank You for Your love and forgiveness. Help us to live our lives for You. Amen.

Leah Rayner

The Only Second Chance That Truly Matters

Read: Luke 15:21–24

During my sophomore year at Pacific Lutheran High School, I was diagnosed with a brain condition called hydrocephalus. Had this gone undetected, it is quite possible I would now be blind. But you know what? At the peak of my despair in this suffering, the good Lord blessed me with a second chance through the support of my friends, family, teachers, and doctors. Because of all these wonderful people, I am able to do all sorts of things that three years ago I could never have dreamed of doing. Through them, God blessed me with a second chance at life.

Time and time again, the Israelites rejected God and His Law, which should have condemned them to death. Yet, time and time again, the Lord showed His everlasting mercy to them and welcomed them back to His loving arms.

Through all the hardships and temptations we face, and all the times we have rejected Him, the Lord gives us a second chance through Christ. He shows us mercy for Christ's sake, just as He was merciful to ancient Israel. As the father warmly welcomed home his lost son, God receives us through Jesus. After Christ bore our shame and suffering on the cross, there was no need to fear God's wrath, for it had been fully carried out on the cross. Praise be to God Almighty, who declared us innocent for Christ's sake!

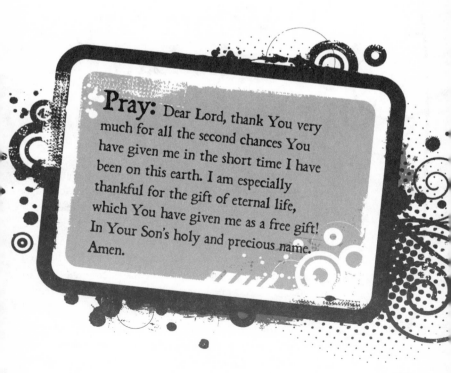

Pray: Dear Lord, thank You very much for all the second chances You have given me in the short time I have been on this earth. I am especially thankful for the gift of eternal life, which You have given me as a free gift! In Your Son's holy and precious name. Amen.

Michael Healy

Maintaining the Law

Read: Leviticus 19:37

Once upon a time, a man was married to a woman who was a perfectionist. No matter what her husband did for her, it was never enough. At the beginning of each day, she made out a list of chores for him to do. At the end of each day, she reviewed the list to make sure he had done all that he was supposed to do. The only compliment he ever received was a grunt if he finished everything on the list. He grew to hate his wife. When she died unexpectedly, he was embarrassed to admit to himself that he was relieved.

Within a year of his wife's death, he met a warm and loving woman who was everything his former wife was not. They fell deeply in love and were married. Every day they spent together seemed better than the day before.

One afternoon, as he was cleaning out boxes in the attic, a crumpled piece of paper caught his eye. It was one of the old chore lists that his first wife had made for him. He could not help reading it again. To his shock and amazement, he discovered that, without even thinking about it, he was now doing for his new wife all the things he used to hate doing for his first wife. His new wife never once suggested that he do any of these chores. He was doing them because he loved her.

Do you ever think that life, for a Christian, is like a list of chores to do? Romans 3:20 reminds us that the Law God gives shows us our sins. But He also gives us the Gospel. As it says in 1 John 4:19, "We love because He first loved us."

The Law breaks us down, but the Gospel restores us in Christ. Law and Gospel work hand in hand. The Gospel is the Good News that God, who created us, also has called and redeemed us in Christ. And the Law, which not only accuses us, also now describes the new life we have in Christ. Those who love Jesus, like the man loved his second wife, are glad to follow God's Law and His Commandments, with the help of the Holy Spirit.

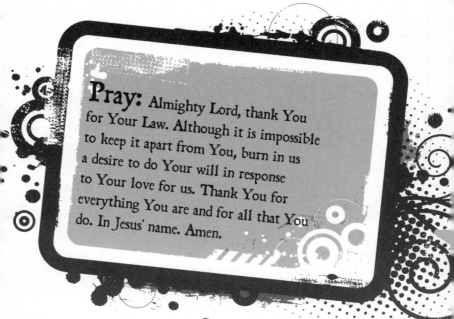

Pray: Almighty Lord, thank You for Your Law. Although it is impossible to keep it apart from You, burn in us a desire to do Your will in response to Your love for us. Thank You for everything You are and for all that You do. In Jesus' name. Amen.

Adam Behmlander

Running the Great Race

Read: John 4:13–14

It was a hot day, and a boy was running in a 5K race. Although he crossed the finish line with a good time, during the race he had become dehydrated, and his body felt weak. The boy had not prepared well for the race.

The day before a race, not the day of, is when you should drink many fluids to keep your body hydrated. If you drink a lot right before the race, you cramp up. This runner was not prepared because he did not hydrate himself properly before the race.

As we run the race of life toward heaven, sin and the devil get in our way. Our starting line is conception, and our finish line is heaven. While in our race, we encounter many difficult obstacles that the devil and the world throw at us in order to slow us down or even to keep us from finishing. We face our own forms of dehydration, and if we do not prepare properly, they can keep us from finishing the race.

Jesus is the living water, the one who keeps us going in the race. When it gets "hot" because of all the obstacles that the devil and the world are throwing at us, and the course gets more difficult, we know that we have God's living water in us and that He is enough to keep us going.

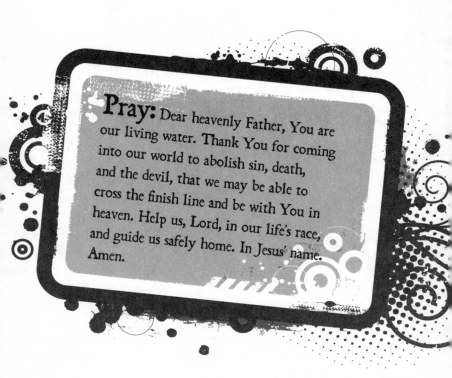

Pray: Dear heavenly Father, You are our living water. Thank You for coming into our world to abolish sin, death, and the devil, that we may be able to cross the finish line and be with You in heaven. Help us, Lord, in our life's race, and guide us safely home. In Jesus' name. Amen.

Kristina Russie

Broken? He Can Fix That

Read: Matthew 11:28

Life is hard. Every day you are faced with some sort of struggle. There are things and people pulling you every which way. You hurt. Maybe your boyfriend dumped you. Maybe your parents are getting a divorce. Maybe you are just really stressed out! What can you do when life gets to be too much? Turn to Jesus.

You are at your wit's end. You have tried everything, and now you just cannot take another step. You are broken and tired. You feel defeated. What can you do? Stop right where you are, bow your head, and ask for strength. Put your trust in the

One who loves you and has promised to help you through. He will not let you down!

We try so hard to take our lives into our own hands. We grit our teeth and pretend we can make it on our own, but there is a better way. Jesus says to us, "Come to Me, all who labor and are heavy laden, and I will give you rest" (Matthew 11:28). He has promised to lift us up when life is tearing us down. He will give us the strength needed to carry on through this hard life. All we need to do is trust Him.

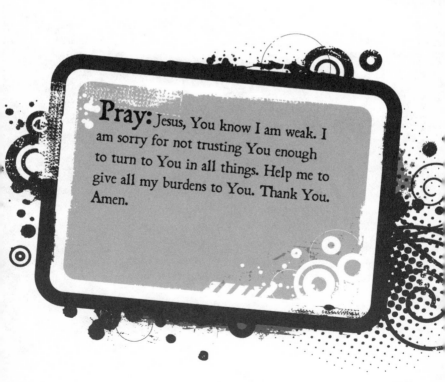

Pray: Jesus, You know I am weak. I am sorry for not trusting You enough to turn to You in all things. Help me to give all my burdens to You. Thank You. Amen.